Key Stage 1 LEARN Writing & Handwriting

NAPE National Association for Primary Education

Contents

AUTHOR: Camilla de la Bédoyère
EDITORIAL: Catherine de la Bédoyère, Quentin de la Bédoyère, John Bolt, Vicky Garrard, Kate Lawson, Sally MacGill, Julia Rolf, Lyndall Willis
DESIGN: Jen Bishop, Dave Jones, Colin Rudderham
ILLUSTRATORS: David Benham, Sarah Wimperis
PRODUCTION: Chris Herbert, Claire Walker
Thanks also to Robert Walster

COMMISSIONING EDITOR: Polly Willis
PUBLISHER AND CREATIVE DIRECTOR: Nick Wells

3 Book Pack ISBN 1-84451-051-4 Book ISBN 1-84451-016-6
6 Book Pack ISBN 1-84451-065-4 Book ISBN 1-84451-074-3
First published in 2003

A copy of the CIP data for this book is available from the British Library upon request.

Created and produced by
FLAME TREE PUBLISHING
Crabtree Hall,
Crabtree Lane,
Fulham, London SW6 6TY
United Kingdom
www.flametreepublishing.com

Flame Tree Publishing is part of The Foundry Creative Media Co. Ltd.

Printed in Croatia

Foreword

Sometimes when I am crossing the playground on my way to visit a primary school I pass young children playing at schools. There is always a stern authoritarian little teacher at the front laying down the law to the unruly group of children in the pretend class. This puzzles me a little because the school I am visiting is very far from being like the children's play. Where do they get this Victorian view of what school is like? Perhaps it's handed down from generation to generation through the genes. Certainly they don't get it from their primary school. Teachers today are more often found alongside their pupils, who are learning by actually doing things for themselves, rather than merely listening and obeying instructions.

Busy children, interested and involved in their classroom reflect what we know about how they learn. Of course they learn from teachers but most of all they learn from their experience of life and their life is spent both in and out of school. Indeed, if we compare the impact upon children of even the finest schools and teachers, we find that three or four times as great an impact is made by the reality of children's lives outside the school. That reality has the parent at the all important centre. No adult can have so much impact, for good or ill, as the young child's mother or father.

This book, and others in the series, are founded on the sure belief that the great majority of parents want to help their children grow and learn and that teachers are keen to support them. The days when parents were kept at arm's length from schools are long gone and over the years we have moved well beyond the white line painted on the playground across which no parent must pass without an appointment. Now parents move freely in and out of schools and very often are found in the classrooms backing up the teachers. Both sides of the partnership know how important it is that children should be challenged and stimulated both in and out of school.

Perhaps the most vital part of this book is where parents and children are encouraged to develop activities beyond those offered on the page. The more the children explore and use the ideas and techniques we want them to learn, the more they will make new knowledge of their very own. It's not just getting the right answer, it's growing as a person through gaining skill in action and not only in books. The best way to learn is to live.

I remember reading a story to a group of nine year old boys. The story was about soldiers and of course the boys, bloodthirsty as ever, were hanging on my every word. I came to the word khaki and I asked the group "What colour is khaki?" One boy was quick to answer. "Silver" he said, "It's silver." "Silver? I queried. "Yes," he said with absolute confidence, "silver, my Dad's car key is silver." Now I reckon I'm a pretty good teller of stories to children but when it came down to it, all my dramatic reading of a gripping story gave way immediately to the power of the boy's experience of life. That meant so much more to him, as it does to all children.

JOHN COE
General Secretary
National Association for Primary Education (NAPE).

NAPE was founded 23 years ago with the aim of improving the quality of teaching and learning in primary schools. The association brings together parents and teachers in partnership.

NAPE National Association for Primary Education

NAPE, Moulton College, Moulton, Northampton, NN3 7RR, Telephone: 01604 647 646 Web: www. nape.org.uk

Writing & Handwriting is one of six books in the **Learn Series** for Key Stage One. These books have been devised to help you support your child as they begin Primary School.

This book introduces you and your child to the National Literacy Strategy and it aims to set out the key skills your child will be learning at school. You should read the book together; your child will need you on hand to guide them through each subject. There are both written and practical activities throughout the book which will help reinforce the concepts that are covered.

You will also find **Parents Start Here** boxes to give you extra information and guidance.

Before you begin any learning session with the book, ensure your child is relaxed and comfortable:

- They should be sitting with their feet touching the floor and their bottom at the back of their seat.
- Put the book at a slight angle so your child can see their pencil point as they write.
- Encourage a good writing grip and neat presentation of work.
- Give your child access to water to drink; research suggests that children who drink water when they work are able to perform better.

Do not attempt to complete too many pages in one sitting; children have short attention spans and you want the experience to remain pleasurable. Offer your child plenty of praise for the work they accomplish. Reinforce the learning with lots of activities away from the book, particularly reading together. Spelling, phonics, reading and writing are all closely related and reinforce one another. It is also essential that your child is developing correct letter formation at this stage, so their creativity is not hampered at a later stage.

There is a checklist at the end of the book; you can use this to show your child how they are progressing. You could introduce a reward system too; children benefit enormously from rewards and praise.

Most importantly, the time you spend together with this book should be enjoyable for both of you.

Parents Start Here...

Neat handwriting is important, not only in itself but for the National Curriculum Tests. Patient coaching and lots of practice will pay great dividends in the future. Check that your child is holding the pencil correctly, otherwise they will always be disadvantaged.

Making Patterns

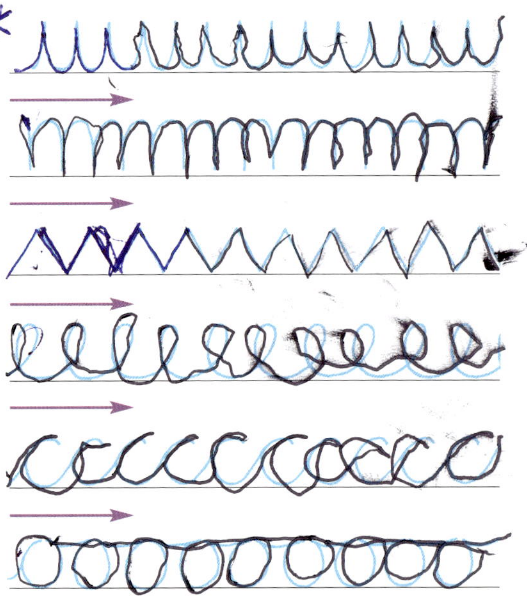

Trace these patterns with your finger, starting at the arrows.
Now trace over them with a pencil, starting at the arrows.
Now copy the patterns. Keep your work neat.

Writing In Comfort

Before you practise your handwriting you must make sure you are sitting comfortably and have the right tools. Hold your pencil like this:

Left-Handers

If your child is left-handed, show them how to sit with their body and paper at a slant to the right. This enables them to see the tip of their pencil, prevents them from smudging their work and helps the movement of the pencil across the page.

7/12/09

Writing Letters

Some letters are small and fit between the lines. Here are some examples for you to copy. Start at the dots.

a a e e s s n n a a e e s s n n

Some letters are taller, and go above the lines. Here are some examples for you to trace and copy:

b b l l h h d d b b l l h h d d

Some letters put their feet down, and stretch below the lines. Here are some examples for you to trace and copy:

g j p y g j p y

Some letters stretch a little way above the line. Trace and then copy them as neatly as you can.

i j t i j t

TRY THIS

Activity

Making models from salt-dough and Plasticine are great ways to make your fingers stronger, which will help your handwriting. Try making alphabet shapes.

Check Your Progress!

Making Patterns ☐

Writing Letters ☐

Turn to page 48 and put a tick next to what you have just learned.

Parents Start Here...

Drawing borders around work provides a good opportunity for children to practise their pencil skills and develop patterns.

Writing Words: Vowels And Consonants

There are 26 letters in the alphabet. Each letter is either a vowel or a consonant, except for one letter, y, which can be either.

Vowels

Vowels have open sounds. Here they are: **a e i o u**

Try saying the vowels without your lips touching.

Here's a little rhyme for you to learn.

a e i o u – You know that I love you.

Consonants

All the other letters in the alphabet, except y, are consonants.
Practise writing these consonants. Trace them first and then copy them.

c m f k p

We need vowels and consonants to make words. For example:

m - a - t

Here are five words where the vowel has been left out. Write in each vowel (a e i o u) in turn, and see the different words you can make, then write out each word in your best handwriting:

b_g

b_g

b_g

b_g

b_g

Write the animal names:

Use a coloured pencil or felt tip pen to draw a ring around all the vowels.

Home Learn

Draw a ring around every vowel you can find:

w r e s u b g h i z o p e

TRY THIS

Activity

Draw a patterned border around these two pages and colour it in.

Check Your Progress!
Vowels And Consonants

Turn to page 48 and put a tick next to what you have just learned.

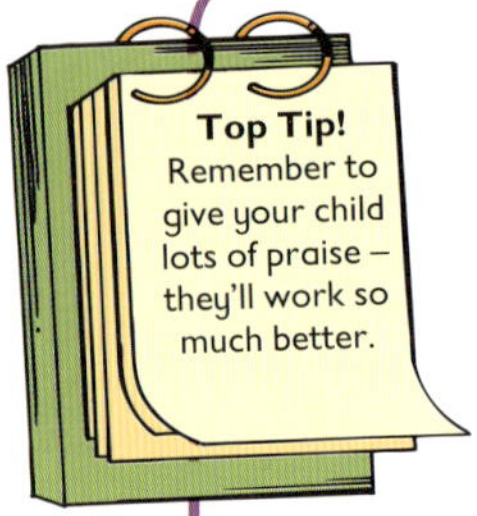

Parents Start Here...

As your child says each word check their pronunciation. e.g. book/food; three/free. If need be, demonstrate mouth movements to help your child notice the differences. Show your child which of their letters/words you are particularly pleased with.

Writing More Words

Now that we've looked at vowels and consonants using simple words, we can look at some more difficult ones.

Adding one letter can completely change a word:

Add an **s** to the beginning of hot, and we get sh**o**t.
Add an **o** to the middle of hot, and we get ho**o**t.
Add an **e** to the end of hat, and we get hat**e**.

Putting in extra letters, or taking letters away, changes the way a word looks, the way it **sounds** and what it **means**.

Try taking away some letters:
From **three** take away an **h**. Write the word you get: ______________

From **tape** take away **t**. Write the word you get: ______________

How can a dog become a cat? Work through this word chain and you will find out:

dog

change **d** to **h** ⟶ ___ ___ ___
change **g** to **t** ⟶ ___ ___ ___
change **o** to **a** ⟶ ___ ___ ___
change **h** to **c** ⟶ ___ ___ ___

cat

Practise writing some words which have consonants and vowels side by side.

First, say the word
Second, copy the word
Third, check that you have copied it well. Put a tick if you have.

three	say	copy		check	☐
hook	say	copy		check	☐
rook	say	copy		check	☐
brook	say	copy		check	☐
book	say	copy		check	☐
sheet	say	copy		check	☐
boo	say	copy		check	☐
bee	say	copy		check	☐

TRY THIS

Activity

Look back at the words you copied on this page and ask yourself how neat your handwriting is. Draw stars next to the best four words.

Check Your Progress!

Writing More Words ☐

Turn to page 48 and put a tick next to what you have just learned.

Parents Start Here...

Don't worry about capital letters, full stops and other simple punctuation yet. We are about to cover it in detail.

Writing Sentences

A sentence is made up of words which tell you about something. Here is an example:

James stroked Thumper.

The sentence has three parts.

Part 1: Who (or what) is the sentence about?
In this example the answer is James.
So James is the subject of the sentence.

Part 2: What did James do? The answer is stroked.
Doing words are called verbs.

Part 3: To whom did James do it? The answer is Thumper.
Thumper is the object of the sentence.

Here are some jumbled words. Put them into order so that they make a sentence, and write it down.

floor washed the the man

Draw a ring around the object in the sentence.

Read these sentences out loud. Use a blue pencil to draw a ring around the (subject) in each sentence.

The dog bit the girl.

The sun shone through the window.

Billy sat on his rabbit.

Rain hits the pavement.

Now use a red pencil to draw rings around the (verbs.) Remember these are the doing words. Ask a grown up to help you if you are not sure. Use a yellow pencil to draw rings around the (objects) in the sentences.

Home Learn

The subjects and objects in these sentences have been underlined for you. Swap them round to make new sentences.

a) The <u>boy</u> jumped on the <u>frog</u>.

The __________ jumped on the __________.

b) The <u>horse</u> chased the <u>hen</u>.

The __________ chased the __________.

c) <u>Giants</u> frighten <u>pixies</u>.

__________ frighten __________.

TRY THIS

Activity

Ask a grown up to put a blindfold on you. Now trace letters in your name in the air and ask the grown up to tell you how well you did.

Check Your Progress!
Writing Sentences

Turn to page 48 and put a tick next to what you have just learned.

Parents Start Here...

Continue to monitor your child's handwriting. If they still struggle to hold a pencil correctly it may be worth investing in a triangular pencil. Keep pencils sharp so your child can see clearly what the pencil point is doing.

Capital Letters And Full Stops

Capital Letters

Sentences always begin with a large letter – a capital letter.

If you look at page 46 you will find all of the capital letters have been written out for you to trace.

Here are some sentences that are missing their first letters. Write the capital letters in. (The little letter has been given to you.)

__he children are playing ball (t)

__orses have hay (h)

__irates love treasure (p)

Capital letters are also used for the names of people and places.

My brother John went to London.

The sentence starts with a capital letter but it also has two names: John and London, so they also have capital letters.

Full Stops

Sentences always (or nearly always) end with a full stop.
Look back at the sentences where you have just put in the capitals and add the full stops.

Home Learn

Here are some sentences that are missing their capital letters and full stops. Write them out, putting in the capital letters and full stops. The names have been underlined to help you.

phil and billy went to spain

martha shops in kwikmart

TRY THIS

Activity

Trace the capital letters on page 46.

Check Your Progress!

Capital Letters And Full Stops

Turn to page 48 and put a tick next to what you have just learned.

Parents Start Here...

Ensure your child does not litter their writing with exclamation marks.

The Friends Of The Full Stop

The full stop has friends.
One of them is the ! exclamation mark

We might use this to show that something surprising is being said:

Matty slid all the way down the hill on his bottom!

Exclamation marks also follow strong commands.

Go to bed!

Another friend of the full stop is the ? question mark

Question marks go at the end of a sentence to show when a question is being asked.

These are all questions:

How old are you?
What is your name?
Do you like lemon sherbets?

Another friend of the full stop is the , comma

Commas are put inside sentences and help us to understand them.

Here is a sentence which needs some commas:

If I broke the window which I never did it wasn't my fault.

Let's try it with commas.

If I broke the window, which I never did, it wasn't my fault.

Commas are also used to separate words in a list of things:

I bought some sausages, bacon, chicken wings and baked beans.

The last two items in a list are always separated by the word and.

Home Learn

Read this example and draw a line from the punctuation marks to their names.

John, a clumsy boy, jumped into a puddle.

Was his mother angry? You bet she was!

question mark   comma   exclamation mark   full stop

TRY THIS

Activity

The comma test: read a sentence out loud and think about where you pause. Those places are probably where you would put a comma.

Check Your Progress!

The Friends Of The Full Stop ☐

Turn to page 48 and put a tick next to what you have just learned.

Practise Your Writing

1. Copy these sentences in your best writing. If you look closely you will see that each sentence uses all the letters in the alphabet.

The quick brown fox jumps over the lazy dog.

The five boxing wizards jumped quickly.

Pack my box with five dozen liquor jugs.

2. Read these sentences below, and see if you can improve them by adding commas. Write the commas in.

a) Yesterday or the day before I went swimming.

b) June and Maggie girls who lived in the same road were always friends.

c) When I went back to school I forgot my pencil case P.E. kit scarf football boots and my hat.

3. Put exclamation marks, full stops or question marks on the ends of these sentences.

a) Stop the train

b) How much do the apples cost

c) I don't really like bananas

d) Did it rain on Wednesday

e) Get me out of here

f) Mice are quite cute

Parents Start Here...

Read poetry and rhymes to your child, and point out more examples. More about poems on page 42.

Words That Rhyme

Read this poem out loud.

Uncle Jim was big and fat
He ate ten meals a day.
Then he exploded just like that,
And bits flew every way.

You will see that the words at the ends of the lines rhyme.
That is, they have the same sound.

Use a coloured pencil to draw rings the two words that rhyme.
Use a different colour to circle two more.

You will see that every line in a poem starts with a capital letter.

Later on we will look at poems again, but here we want to see how rhyming can help us to say words correctly.

Here is a list of words with a rhyming word. Find another rhyming word and write it in. The first one is done for you.

beg peg leg

sat cat

den pen

fun bun

Read this out loud:

It would be good
If only I could
Have some more food.

Good rhymes with could, but it doesn't rhyme with food, although food has the same vowels as good. So rhyming can be tricky.

Home Learn

Here are some pairs of words. If they rhyme put a tick in the answer box.

☐ pain drain	☐ speak break	☐ hook rook
☐ feel peal	☐ seal real	☐ book shoot

TRY THIS

Activity

Choose some poetry books from your local library. You may be able to find some that come with tapes – and then you can read the words while listening to the poems.

Check Your Progress!
Words That Rhyme ☐

Turn to page 48 and put a tick next to what you have just learned.

Parents Start Here...

If necessary, ask questions like 'what kind of man is he?' Ask your child to think of alternative adjectives to the ones they have chosen. For adverbs, ask questions like: 'How is the mouse squeaking?' Ask your child to think of alternative adverbs to the ones they have chosen.

Describing Words

There are two kinds of describing words.

Adjectives describe people or things.
Adverbs describe doing words (remember that verbs are doing words, like run, walk or shout).

Describing People Or Things

Look at the pictures below.
Choose good adjectives from the list to complete the sentences.

Adjectives: funny full hairy tall smelly kind quiet

This is a ________________ man.

Look at the ________________ monkey.

My wastepaper basket is ________________.

Describing Verbs

Words that describe verbs (doing words) are called adverbs. You can remember the name because it is like verb. Adverbs often end in –ly.

The boy ran quickly.

Ran is the verb in this sentence.
How did he run? He ran quickly.
Quickly is the adverb in this sentence.

Home Learn

Look at the pictures below. Choose good adverbs from the list to complete the sentences.

Adverbs: angrily boastfully excitedly helpfully quietly

This mouse squeaks ______________________.

Mum slammed the door ______________________.

I opened my presents ______________________.

TRY THIS

Activity

Listen carefully when people talk. Try to identify the verbs they use in their sentences. You may even hear some adverbs, if you listen carefully enough.

Check Your Progress!

Describing Words ☐

Turn to page 48 and put a tick next to what you have just learned.

Parents Start Here...

Help your child clap to the syllables in long words. This aids in the 'chopping' of words. When your child reads to you, encourage the chopping habit to tackle longer words. You will quickly find that being able to read the first part of a word often gives the child enough of a clue to correctly guess the whole word.

Chopping Up Long Words

Reading long words can be hard.
Chopping them into smaller words may help.

notebook .... note book

landslide .... land slide.

Here are some words you can chop.
Write out the two little words which make up the longer word.

Armchair ________ ________

Fireplace ________ ________

Inside ________ ________

Your chopped up pieces do not have to be real words,
as long as you can read them.

This long word can be chopped into pieces that make it easier to read:

Hexagon .... hex a gon

Here are some more words you can chop. Show how you have chopped the words and say them out loud.

Sister ______________

Camera ______________

Handkerchief ____________

Home Learn

Draw lines through these words to show how you might chop them up:

Vampire

Wizard

Witch

Monster

Zombie

TRY THIS

Activity

Try saying some long words and clap along to them as you do. Ask a grown up to help you think of the words.

Check Your Progress!

Chopping Up Long Words ☐

Turn to page 48 and put a tick next to what you have just learned.

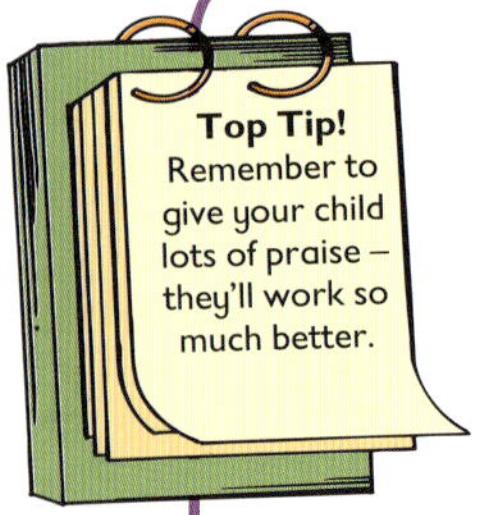

Parents Start Here...

Provide your child with an exercise book or notebook. Encourage your child to write down new words they read or hear. Return to the Word Book frequently for a quick recap. This is a good habit which will be needed throughout school. You can help your child start sections titled 'adjectives' and 'adverbs'.

Keeping A Word Book

All the time, even when we are quite old, we keep meeting new words. What do they mean? How do we say them? How do we write them? It's a good idea to keep a Word Book.

Let's get started with some words from our daily lives. See how many words you can add to the list.

Words At Home

staircase
oven
microwave
saucepan
television
computer
lounge

____
____
____
____
____

Words In The Street

shop
traffic
supermarket
plastic bag
pavement
level crossing
bus stop

____
____
____
____
____

Don't forget to chop up words if you find them difficult.

Animals

tiger
giraffe
tortoise
crocodile
goose
elephant
reindeer
hippopotamus

Names

Margaret
Manchester
Grandpa
Uncle
Brighton
New York
Christmas
Thomas

Words At School

classroom
teacher
exercise book
revision
homework
assembly
reception

TRY THIS

Activity

Copy some of your new words, or ones you find hard to say, in your Word Book.

Check Your Progress!

Keeping A Word Book

Turn to page 48 and put a tick next to what you have just learned.

Parents Start Here...

Together with your child try to think of some alternatives to 'nice'.

Really Useful Words

Words That Mean The Opposite

What is the opposite of kind? Unkind, of course.
Many words have their opposites.
Write in the opposite in the space:

handsome = not handsome = ______________

rough = not rough = ______________

tidy = not tidy = ______________

Sometimes we can find more than one word for the opposite. That gives us a choice, and we can pick the best one to show what we want to say.
For example:
The opposites for kind could be unkind, cruel, selfish.

See if you can find two opposites for each of the words below.

tidy ______________ ______________

quickly ______________ ______________

loudly ______________ ______________

Words That Mean The Same

On the last page we saw three words that mean very similar things: unkind, cruel, selfish.

Similar means nearly the same. Put it into your Word Book.

Home Learn

Each row of words has three words that are similar and one that means something different. Ring the odd one out.

a) nasty lovely unpleasant disgusting

b) trapeze friendly pleasant polite

c) scared frightened calm terrified

d) difficult hard violet complicated

e) angry happy content relaxed

TRY THIS

Activity

When you tell someone a story, try to use some of the words in your Word Book.

Check Your Progress!

Really Useful Words ☐

Turn to page 48 and put a tick next to what you have just learned.

Activities

1. Follow the wiggly lines to find the rhyming words:

horse hail cuff fur

her rough course pale

2. Find the adjectives in this word search.
Remember that adjectives describe people or things.

s	b	s	m	a	l	l
a	i	r	u	u	i	i
d	g	l	i	g	t	g
b	t	a	l	l	t	h
l	s	t	o	y	l	t
u	k	e	n	r	e	d
e	a	c	g	o	o	d

sad
long
red
silly
little
light
ugly
small
tall
big
blue
good
late

3. Use the words you are given to put an adverb into each of these sentences. You can add –ly to make the words into adverbs.
Remember: an adverb is a word that describes a verb (doing word).

a) The boy tip-toed __________ into the classroom. (quiet)
b) Little chicks chirp __________ in their nests. (loud)
c) Tortoises creep along the ground __________. (slow)
d) The naughty children behave __________ when the teacher goes out of the room. (terrible)
e) The dancer tiptoed __________ across the stage. (graceful)

Parents Start Here...

Point out signs and notices to your child. Help them to think about the way signs and notices are presented – styles, typefaces and colours. You could help your child make a notice on the computer.

Signs

Signs tell us about something we need to know immediately.

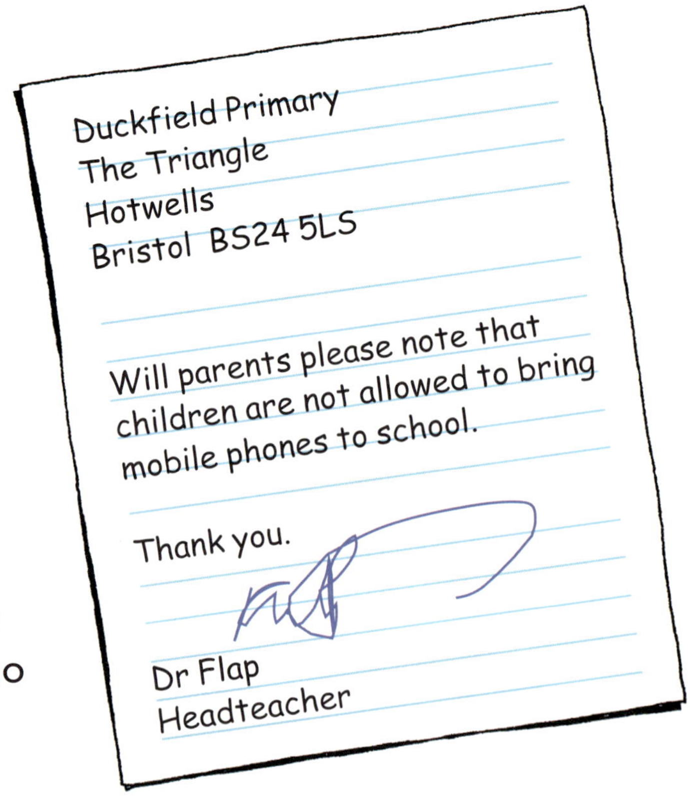

Duckfield Primary
The Triangle
Hotwells
Bristol BS24 5LS

Will parents please note that children are not allowed to bring mobile phones to school.

Thank you.

Dr Flap
Headteacher

Notices

Notices are like longer signs.
They are often given out to the people who need to read them.

When you write an address you must use capital letters for the beginning of street names, towns, cities and countries.

Instructions

Instructions tell us how to do something. For instance, if you buy a toy or a game, you will usually find instructions telling you how to make it work.

- It is important to read instructions carefully.
- It is important to write instructions so that they can easily be understood.

Here is an example:

An address on an envelope is an instruction to the postman or postwoman. It tells them how to find your home.

Home Learn

Use your best handwriting and colouring-in to complete this sign.

TRY THIS

Activity

Learn how to write your own address on to an envelope then send yourself a letter in the post.

Check Your Progress!

Signs ☐

Turn to page 48 and put a tick next to what you have just learned.

Top Tip!
Learning is fun, so if your child is tired, let them come back to this when they are fresh.

Parents Start Here...

When you get to the Home Learn question, ask your child why they selected this particular book. Ask them for concrete reasons for their choice. This is hard for a child, but now is the time to start developing a critical sense.

Books

Story Books

Hopefully your bedroom shelves are full of great story books, which are packed with adventures, fantastic places and fascinating people. Books that tell made-up stories are called fiction.

Non-Fiction Books

These are books about facts. They are not made-up stories.

A biography is a book that tells us about someone's life. Which of these books is a biography?

Reference Books

These are books which you look in to find a fact.

Dictionaries

These tell you the meanings of words and how to spell them.

Encyclopedias

These have lots of information about people, places and things.

Telephone Directories

These give telephone numbers and addresses.

Home Learn

Write the name of your favourite fiction book.

____

Who is the author?______________________________

The author of the book is the person who wrote it.
Put this word into your Word Book.

TRY THIS

Activity

You have come across lots of new words on these two pages. Put them into your Word Book. Write down their meanings.

Check Your Progress!

Books ☐

Turn to page 48 and put a tick next to what you have just learned.

Parents Start Here...

Ask your child questions about their favourite story. It is important for them to see the basic structure of 'characters and plot', which all stories share.

Stories

We all know the story of Cinderella. She started off being miserable. Then along came a Fairy Godmother who sent her to the ball, where she met Prince Charming and fell in love. But Cinderella made a silly mistake, leaving after midnight, and she was miserable again. It all ended happily ever after when Prince Charming found her.

The main character in the story is Cinderella, but there are other characters, too. In our minds we see the characters as real people, and we care about what is going to happen to them.

Write in the names of some of the other characters in the story.

On page 33 you wrote down the name of your favourite fiction book. Who are the main characters in your favourite book?
Write their names here:

______________________ ______________________

______________________ ______________________

The story of what happens to the characters is called the plot or the storyline. A good plot makes you want to read the story. A boring plot will make you want to put the book down.

Home Learn

What was the plot of your favourite fiction book? Write down five things that happened in the story. Remember to write the ending.

1 ______________________

2 ______________________

3 ______________________

4 ______________________

5 ______________________

TRY THIS

Activity

Make up three characters you could use in a story. Give them names, ages, habits (good and bad ones!). Think about what they look like and sound like.

Check Your Progress!

Stories ☐

Turn to page 48 and put a tick next to what you have just learned.

Parents Start Here...

If your child lacks the writing skill to put down a whole story on paper don't worry. Let your child tell you the story and you can write it down, letting your child put in the occasional sentence.

Writing Your Own Story

Would you like to try writing a little story? Here is an example:

Whatever Charlie was doing, he was always thinking of something else. If he were tying his shoelaces he'd be thinking about his scooter. If he were on his scooter he'd be thinking about ice cream. He simply could not keep his mind in one place.

One day he went down to the sweetshop and chose himself a bag of sweets. But he was thinking about his Mum's new hat, so he walked out without paying.

Mr Grimes, the shopkeeper, ran out after him, shouting "Come back, you nasty little thief!"

Charlie ran home as fast as he could, with Mr Grimes at his heels. Luckily his Dad was at the garden gate, and, when Mr Grimes complained, he explained that Charlie would never steal anything. It was just that he was thinking about something else. Mr Grimes wasn't pleased, but he understood. Was Charlie sorry for what he had done? We don't know. Charlie was thinking about something else.

TRY THIS

Activity

Using a sheet of lined paper, have a go at writing a story. Use your best handwriting, and cross out mistakes neatly. To get you going, you can try this as a beginning:

It was a very cold day. The snow was lying thick on the ground and the ponds were frozen hard. Jo decided it was a good day for exploring.

Check Your Progress!
Writing Your Own Story

Turn to page 48 and put a tick next to what you have just learned.

Parents Start Here...

Show your child how to make neat amendments to their work. Generally, teachers prefer their pupils to put a cross through their work rather than rub it out.

Improving Your Story

When you read a good story you find yourself pulled right inside it. You imagine the characters as real people. When you are writing a story you must help your reader to see it inside their heads. One important way is to use describing words – adjectives and adverbs.

Look back at pages 20 and 21 to remind yourself about adverbs and adjectives.

Tick ✓ the most interesting sentence.

☐ Maggie lived in a house by the forest.

☐ Maggie lived alone in a gloomy house, near the haunted forest.

Cross out the wrong answers:

Alone is an adverb/adjective
Gloomy is an adverb/adjective
Haunted is an adverb/adjective

Here are three sentences.
Choose one of the adjectives suggested and write it in the space:

He walked down the ____________ road. long, narrow, busy

Grandad went into the ____________ room. dark, cold, green

Jon looked up and saw the ____________ sky. grey, bright, cloudy

Home Learn

Circle the adverbs in these sentences.

As the mongoose ran hurriedly across the hot desert sand she was searching. She looked quickly, from left to right, trying to find somewhere to hide. The golden eagle swooped gracefully overhead, its talons silently opening, ready to grab the little creature.

TRY THIS

Activity

Now look at the story you wrote and see if you can find places for good adjectives and adverbs.

Check Your Progress!
Improving Your Story ☐
Turn to page 48 and put a tick next to what you have just learned.

Parents Start Here...

Once you have read through this account, help your child to pick out what he or she has learnt about the grandmother, and how the account shows respect, love and trust without saying so directly. Encourage your child to make notes before starting a composition. This will oblige them to think before they write – a quality they will need for the future.

Word Pictures Of People

How would you describe your best friend? You might want to say something about their appearance (what they look like) but also – and perhaps more importantly – what sort of person they are. You can create a word picture of them. Here is an example:

My grandmother had her 70th birthday today, but she looks much younger than that. She looks quite grand, except that her glasses keep slipping down her nose. She is rather strict, and we have to behave well when we visit her. But she is also very kind, and she spends lots of time playing games and talking with me. She knows about many things because she's lived a long time. Sometimes she repeats her stories because she's forgotten what she has already said. She tells me about birds and animals and flowers, which I love. I can talk to her about anything, and she listens. If I ever had a real problem, even if I'd done something bad, I'd go to my grandmother, and she'd always be able to help.

Does that give you a word picture of the grandmother? Do you think you'd like to meet her, or would you prefer not to? Because it's about a real person we get a mixed picture, because human beings all have good and bad things about them.

TRY THIS

Activity

Choose someone you know at school and write a word picture about them. Use lined paper, and your best handwriting. Before you start you might make some notes of the main things you want to say. This will help you to write your word picture clearly.

Before you begin your word picture, make some notes and jot down some good adjectives you think you might be able to use.

Check Your Progress!
Word Pictures Of People

Turn to page 48 and put a tick next to what you have just learned.

Parents Start Here...

You may need to demonstrate rhythm by clapping to the poems. Some children, like dancers, have a natural ear for rhythm; others will find it more difficult.

Poems

Poems started as songs. They were easy to remember, and they could tell a story, or show your feelings, or make the reader think hard. Some poems can be very long, but often they are quite short. Here is an example of a very short poem:

My kitten is a curled up ball
When he's fast asleep,
But he turns into a tiger
When you see him leap.

Notice that poems use ordinary punctuation, like full stops and commas, but each line begins with a capital letter.

Rhyme

Poems do not have to rhyme, but they often do. So it's best to start with rhyming poems. Which lines rhyme in the poem above?

Home Learn

In the poem below, write in a rhyming word in the blank spaces. The two lines marked a should rhyme with each other and the lines marked b should rhyme with each other.

a My dog prefers to lie on chairs
b Where I can stroke his head,
a But follows when I go ______________
b And sleeps upon my ______________.

Rhythm

Poems have rhythm – which is easier to show than to explain. Here are two tiny poems. See which one you prefer.

Hear the fluffy ducklings quack
When they want their mother back.

and

Hear the fluffy ducklings quack
They always seem to want their mother back.

In the first poem the sound of the two lines balance each other. That's rhythm.

TRY THIS

Activity

Discover the rhythm in these poems by tapping your finger as you say the words or sounds.

Check Your Progress!

Poems ☐

Turn to page 48 and put a tick next to what you have just learned.

Parents Start Here...

Ensure your child leaves spaces between paragraphs when they copy the letter and help them to keep their writing neat. Keep a watchful eye for the correct letter formation – bad habits developed now will be very difficult to break later on.

Handwriting Practice

Here are some reminders to help you keep your handwriting looking neat and presentable at all times.

- Always hold your pencil properly.
- Leave a space between words. Put your finger between words to help you leave the correct space.
- If you make a mistake cross it through neatly.
- Keep your pencils sharp so you can always see the point.
- Use capital letters at the beginning of sentences and for names.

Home Learn

Copy this letter in your best handwriting. Read it through first.

Dear Annie,

Thank you for inviting me to your birthday party. I love going to the cinema so I am really pleased you asked me to come with you. My Mum says I can go back to your house for tea afterwards.

Would you like to come to my house for a sleepover on Saturday?

Lots of love,

Katie

TRY THIS

Activity

Draw a patterned border around these pages and colour it in.

Check Your Progress!

Handwriting Practice ☐

Turn to page 48 and put a tick next to what you have just learned.

Activities

A B C D E F G

H I J K L M N

O P Q R S T U

V W X y Z

a b c d e f g h

i j k l m n o p

q r s t u v w x y z

Answers

Page 7
Home Learn
e u i o e

Page 8
Words to make up the chain are: dog, hog, hot, hat, cat

Page 10
The man washed the floor.
Floor is the object.

Page 11
The subjects are:
dog
sun
Billy
Rain

The verbs are:
bit
shone
sat
hits

The objects are:
girl
window
rabbit
pavement

Home Learn
a) The frog jumped on the boy.
b) The hen chased the horse.
c) Pixies frighten giants.

Page 13
Home Learn
Phil and Billy went to Spain.
Martha shops in Kwikmart.

Page 17
2. a) Yesterday, or the day before, I went swimming.
b) June and Maggie, girls who lived in the same road, were always friends.
c) When I went back to school I forgot my pencil, case, P.E. kit, scarf, football boots and my hat.
3. a) Stop the train!
b) How much do the apples cost?
c) I don't really like bananas.
d) Did it rain on Wednesday?
e) Get me out of here!
f) Mice are quite cute.

Page 18
The rhyming pairs:
fat and that, day and way

Page 19
Home Learn
Rhyming pairs are: pain/drain, feel/peal, seal/real, hook/rook.

Page 20
Adjectives:
This is a tall man.
Look at the hairy monkey.
My wastepaper basket is full.

Page 21
Home Learn
This mouse squeaks quietly.
Mum angrily slammed the door.
I opened my presents excitedly.

Page 22
Chopped words:
arm + chair
fire + place
in + side

Page 23
sis + ter
cam + er + a
hand + ker + chief
Home Learn
vam/pire
wiz/ard
wit/ch
mon/ster
zom/bie

Page 26
Opposites:
handsome/ugly
rough/smooth
tidy/untidy

More opposites:
tidy: untidy/messy
quickly: slowly/lazily
loudly: quietly/silently

Page 27
Home Learn
a) lovely
b) trapeze
c) calm
d) violet
e) angry

Page 28
1. horse – course
hail – pale
cuff – rough
fur – her

2.

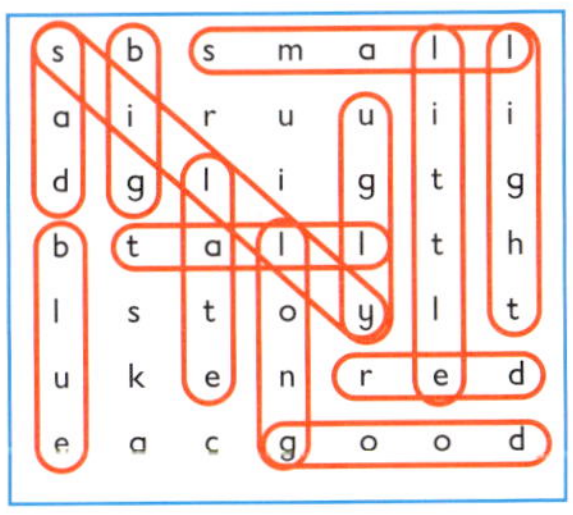

3. a) The boy tip-toed quietly into the classroom.
b) Little chicks chirp loudly in their nests.
c) Tortoises creep along the ground slowly.
d) The naughty children behave terribly when the teacher goes out of the room.
e) The dancer tiptoed gracefully across the stage.

Page 32
Biography = The Life of Queen Elizabeth I

Page 34
Other characters: Ugly sisters, Prince Charming, Fairy Godmother.

Page 39
Alone is an adverb
Gloomy is an adjective
Haunted is an adjective

Home Learn
As the mongoose ran hurriedly across the hot desert sand she was searching. She looked quickly, from left to right, trying to find somewhere to hide. The golden eagle swooped gracefully overhead, its talons silently opening, ready to grab the little creature.

Page 43
Home Learn
My dog prefers to lie on chairs
Where I can stroke his head,
But follows when I go upstairs
And sleeps upon my bed.

Check Your Progress!

- Making Patterns ☐
- Writing Letters ☐
- Vowels And Consonants ☐
- Writing More Words ☐
- Writing Sentences ☐
- Capital Letters And Full Stops ☐
- The Friends Of The Full Stop ☐
- Words That Rhyme ☐
- Describing Words ☐
- Chopping Up Long Words ☐
- Keeping A Word Book ☐
- Really Useful Words ☐
- Signs ☐
- Books ☐
- Stories ☐
- Writing Your Own Story ☐
- Improving Your Story ☐
- Word Pictures Of People ☐
- Poems ☐
- Handwriting Practice ☐